Matchstick Mini and otl

By Edel Malone

Original concept created, illustrated, and written by Edel Malone. I'm sure you will love these books as much as I do. I know you will enjoy making lasting memories with your child moving forward in all stages of their lives by encouraging your child to tell you what's on their mind throughout their lifetime. Asking questions is the way forward. Check out the other Matchstick Mini books from this series.

https://lifestylethoughts.ie/

The Matchstick Mini book series has been designed to encourage your child to open up and talk about what is on their mind. The topics covered are related to young children to encourage good communication techniques carrying on into each stage of their lives, keeping kindness, manners and values in mind.

OTHER BOOKS FROM THIS SERIES

Matchstick Mini and safety

Matchstick Mini has fun

Matchstick Mini and school

Matchstick Mini is very clever

Matchstick is very good

Matchstick Mini is healthy

Matchstick Mini always tells the person who is minding him where he is going. Matchstick Mini does not want people to worry if he got lost, he is very clever.

Matchstick Mini knows if everyone liked the same things it would be very boring. Matchstick Mini knows that not everyone likes the same things, he knows that it is okay for everyone to like different things. Liking different things is good.

Matchstick Mini is not jealous of other people, he knows that everyone is different. Matchstick Mini knows that everyone looks different and everyone likes different things, he loves that everyone is not the same.

Matchstick Mini likes to share, he likes to share his toys with his friends and family, he likes that everyone has different toys and he thinks playing with different toys is fun. Matchstick Mini also likes to play on his own too, he likes to be happy and have fun.

Matchstick Mini loves to see his friends. Matchstick Mini and his friends all have different types of days, he loves to listen to his friends talking about their day and he likes to tell his friends about his day too.

Matchstick Mini is kind to others. Matchstick Mini knows if someone looks sad, he likes to be kind to others when they look sad. Are you always kind to other people, is everyone kind to you?

Matchstick Mini loves animals, he would never hurt an animal. Matchstick Mini knows that hurting an animal is not good. Matchstick Mini likes animals, his favorite animal is a cat. What is your favorite animal?

Matchstick Mini knows that everyone speaks differently, he likes that everyone does not sound the same. Matchstick Mini loves that no two people look or sound the same, he thinks everyone being different is good.

Matchstick Mini loves his family, he knows that all families are not the same and that's okay, he thinks being different is good. Matchstick Mini loves that everyone is different, do you like that everyone is different?

Matchstick Mini knows that everyone moves around in different ways, some people have cars and some don't, some people have a wheelchair, some people have a walking stick and some people don't and that's okay. Matchstick Mini thinks being different is good, he loves that everyone is not the same.

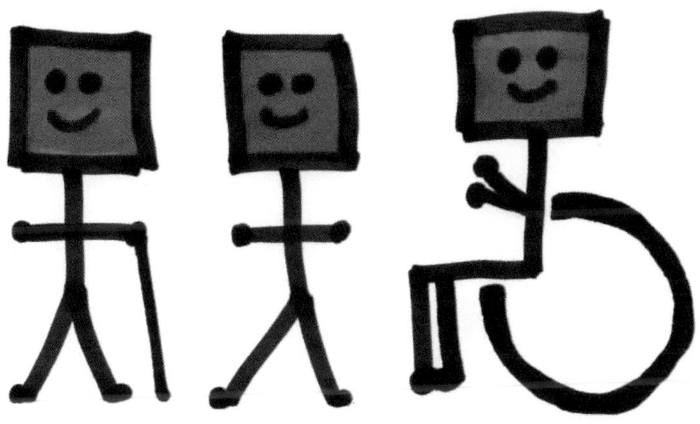

Matchstick Mini loves that everyone is different shapes, different sizes, and different colors, he knows that some people have lots of hair, some people have long hair, short hair and some people have no hair. Some people have black hair, brown hair, pink hair, grey hair, he thinks that being different is good.

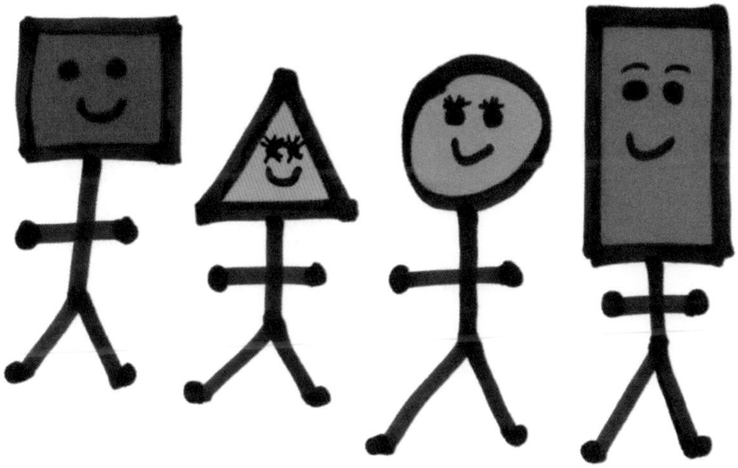

Matchstick Mini knows that everyone looks different, he knows that he looks different from all of his friends, he thinks being different is good. Matchstick Mini loves that everyone looks different, do you like that everyone looks different too?

Matchstick Mini loves to go and visit his family and friends. When he visits other people's homes, he has respect for other people's homes. Matchstick Mini will try not to break anything or leave a mess, he loves that everyone else's home looks different from his home. Matchstick Mini loves when his friends and family come to visit him too, they have lots of fun.

Matchstick Mini loves his home, he knows that everyone has different homes, some people live in houses, some people live in apartments and he loves that everyone's home is different. Matchstick Mini loves to visit other people's homes, he likes to see different places too.

Printed in Great Britain
by Amazon